W9-ACC-558

ANIMAL BEHAVIOR REVEALED

HOW ANIMALS FEEL

REBECCA STEFOFF

Cavendish
Square

New York

This book is dedicated to HENRY BERTRAM LONGSTOCKING BARRIOS.

Published in 2014 by Cavendish Square Publishing, LLC
303 Park Avenue South, Suite 1247, New York, NY 10010

Library of Congress Cataloging-in-Publication Data
Stefoff, Rebecca, 1951-
How animals feel / Rebecca Stefoff.
p. cm. • (Animal behavior revealed)
Includes bibliographical references and index.
Summary: "Provides comprehensive information on how animals feel by citing examples of
emotional understanding and providing examples of animal altruism"—Provided by publisher.
ISBN 978-1-60870-511-5 (hardcover) • ISBN 978-1-62712-022-7 (paperback) • ISBN 978-1-60870-613-6 (ebook)
1. Emotions in animals—Juvenile literature. 2. Animal behavior—Juvenile literature. I. Title. II. Series.
QL785.27.S74 2013 • 91.5 • dc22 • 2010053239

Art Director: Anahid Hamparian • Series Designer: Alicia Mikles

Photo research by Laurie Platt Winfrey, Carousel Research, Inc.

The photographs in this book are used by permission and through the courtesy of:
Cover: Minden Pictures/ Mitsuaki Iwago; *Associated Press:* 21; *AGEfotostock:* Stephen Krasemann, 20; J. Bauer/
Mauritius Images, 32; J. Kottmann/Blickwinkel, 54; *Alamy:* Simon Colmar & Abby Rex, 43; Juniors Bildarchiv,
65; *DPA Picture Alliance:* 25; *ElephantVoices.org,:* Joyce Poole 36; *Getty Images:* Time & Life Pictures, 7; George
Grail/ National Geographic, 52; Oxford Scientific, 61; *Glow Images:* 28; *The Gorilla Foundation:* Ron Cohn, 26;
Courtesy Great Ape Trust: 34; *Minden Pictures:* Doug Perrine/NPL, 15; Anup Shah, 17, 63; Fabio Liverani, 39;
Richard du Toit, 66; *Newscom:* s70/Zuma Press, 19; *Photo Researchers:* Richard Hanson, 59; *Robert L. Pitman:* 4.
Joy Rexroat, DMV: 10; *State Museum of Natural History, Stuttgart:* 48; *Superstock:* Imagebroker.net, 45.

Printed in the United States of America

CONTENTS

INVESTIGATING ANIMAL BEHAVIOR

Why does an elk save the life of a small rodent that is drowning in a water trough? When a female elephant stands for a day and a night over the body of her calf that has just died, nuzzling it with her trunk, is she grieving? Is a dog happy when it is wagging its tail? Do animals have feelings—and if they do, can science help us understand them?

Scientists are exploring the subject of emotions in the animal world in all kinds of ways. Their experiments range from watching ants rescue relatives buried by sand, to testing the memories of fish, to building mirrors big enough, and sturdy enough, for full-grown elephants and killer whales to see their reflections. Recent research into animals' feelings has answered some questions about the creatures that share our world, and it has raised new questions.

An elk rescues a drowning marmot in an Idaho zoo. Did the elk feel sorry for the marmot? Did it want to keep its drinking water free of dead rodents? Whatever the reason, the elk was gentle with the small marmot, which recovered and went on its way.

People have always been fascinated by animals. Tens of thousands of years ago, our ancestors painted lifelike pictures of bears, bison, and deer on cave walls. Twenty-five centuries ago, Greek thinkers wrote about animals and their habits. Those writings were the beginning of **zoology**, the scientific study of animals.

In time zoologists began to wonder why animals do the things they do. When a whale saves a seal's life, for example, is the whale acting out of **instinct**—a built-in pattern of behavior that is programmed into its genes—or does the whale feel sympathy for the seal? Questions like these led to **ethology**, the branch of zoology that studies animal behavior.

Ethology was established as a science in the twentieth century. One of its pioneers was Konrad Lorenz of Austria, who studied the behavior of geese and ducks. When these birds hatch they usually see their mother right away, and after that they follow her around. Lorenz wondered what would happen if young birds hatched apart from others of their **species**. He experimented with geese and found that newly hatched birds bonded with the first thing they saw. When geese first saw Lorenz after they hatched, they bonded with him and followed him around as if he were their mother. Lorenz called this behavior imprinting.

Konrad Lorenz learned about animal behavior by studying geese and ducks. In this 1955 photo, Lorenz is trailed by young birds that imprinted on him as soon as they hatched.

Lorenz published his findings in 1935. The next year he met Niko-
laas Tinbergen, a Dutch zoologist who was also curious about how animals react to signals from their environment. Tinbergen and Lorenz
studied seagulls and ducks together. They discovered that young birds
raised by humans showed no fear of round or square cardboard cutouts, but they instinctively recognized dangerous shapes. The birds
became afraid when cutouts shaped like hawks and eagles flew over
their nests, even though they had never seen those **predators** before.

The work of Lorenz and Tinbergen was a step toward understanding animal instincts. In 1973 the two men shared a Nobel Prize, one
of the highest scientific honors in the world, for their work in the new
science of animal behavior.

Tinbergen warned other scientists against **anthropomorphism**,
which is a fancy way of saying "giving human qualities to animals."
When we describe animals in human terms, such as saying, "Oh, that
bear is sad," we are anthropomorphizing.

For a long time, anthropomorphism was strictly forbidden in ethology. In recent years, though, scientists have learned much about the
inner lives of animals—how they think, feel, communicate, and play.
As scientists discover more similarities between humans and other
animals, some experts take a less strict view of anthropomorphism.
Thinking that animals are completely different from people may be
as big a mistake as thinking that animals are just like people.

The study of animal behavior takes many forms. Some researchers focus on **psychology**, the study of human and animal minds, or on
evolution, the history of life on Earth. **Sociobiologists** study animals

that live in social groups, such as ants and prairie dogs. Behavioral ecologists look at how animals interact with their environments. Other researchers investigate animal communication and **intelligence**.

This book explores the emotional lives of animals. It looks at scientific research into animals' feelings and the ways they understand the world. We will never be able to fully understand what goes on inside animals' minds, but these discoveries are changing the way we look at the creatures around us.

1. INSTINCTS AND ACTIONS

When scientists went looking for a pack of killers, they found something unexpected—animals saving the lives of other animals.

In January 2009, in the middle of the Antarctic summer, a group of biologists set sail from South America on a vessel called the *Golden Fleece*. Their mission was to study orcas in the cold waters near Antarctica. Orcas are large black-and-white whales that are sometimes called killer whales or "wolves of the sea" because they are predators that hunt in packs, like wolves. The scientists hoped to film a hunting technique used by orcas to catch seals that live on and around ice floes, which are chunks of floating ice. When orcas spot a seal sitting on a floe, they sometimes line up close together and swim toward the floe. This creates a big wave that may wash the seal off the ice and into an orca's jaws.

The team of scientists came upon ten orcas surrounding two adult humpback whales. Pods, or groups, of orcas sometimes harass larger

An orca or killer whale circles a chunk of ice where a seal has taken refuge from the predator. In the background a larger humpback whale swims onto the scene. To the surprise of scientists who watched from a research ship, this drama ended with two humpbacks saving the seal from a pod of orcas.

whales such as humpbacks, looking for signs of weakness to attack. These humpbacks were hitting the water with their tails and flippers while roaring through their blowholes. The big whales seemed upset, but the scientists aboard the *Golden Fleece* saw no sign that they were under attack.

Watching videos of the encounter, the scientists noticed a seal between the two humpbacks. What was the seal doing there? It wasn't the humpbacks' **prey**. Humpback whales are not hunters—they eat tiny shrimp, fish, and other small creatures that they filter out of the seawater with their comb-like teeth. The scientists decided that the seal had swum between the humpbacks to get away from the orcas, and that the orcas were harassing the humpbacks because they wanted the seal.

Soon the orca pod moved on, leaving the humpbacks and the seal behind. The scientists followed them. The orcas located a different seal on an ice floe and made a wave that split the floe into pieces. This left the seal stranded on a piece of ice not much bigger than its body. The scientists later wrote about what happened next:

> Just when it seemed the killers were about to have their way, the same pair of humpback whales charged in, swimming around the floe, bellowing and thrashing the water. The killer whales seemed annoyed and finally left the seal alone, still safe on the floe.

A week later, the scientists saw a different pod of orcas attack a seal on an ice floe. This time the killer whales succeeded in washing the seal into the water. Two large humpback whales—not the same ones the scientists had seen before—joined the fight. The seal swam toward the humpbacks as fast as it could. The scientists thought that the seal was hoping to hide from the attacking orcas next to the whales' enormous bodies.

When the seal got close to one of the humpbacks, the humpback rolled over onto its back. Rushing water carried the seal up onto the whale's chest. The orcas charged, but the humpback arched its back to raise its chest up out of the water—and out of the orcas' reach. Water streaming down from the humpback's chest almost washed the seal away, but the humpback used a flipper to gently move the seal back to the safety of its raised chest. Protected from the orcas, the seal soon made its way onto an ice floe and out of danger.

Three times in one week the scientists on the *Golden Fleece* saw humpback whales protect seals from hunting orcas. Why did the humpbacks get involved? Did they feel sorry for the seals? Were they angry at the orcas?

Questions such as these run the risk of anthropomorphism, or, as noted earlier, thinking that animals do the things they do because they have feelings and reactions like our own. However, there is another possible explanation for the whales' behavior: instinct.

Animal Instincts

Scientists used to think that animals were like machines. In the seventeenth century, French thinker René Descartes called animals "automatons" (an early word for robots). In his view, animals did not think or feel or make decisions. Instead, they acted in a rigid, un-changing way because they were born with a set of basic instructions built into their animal nature.

Those "instructions" are now known as instincts. Dogs bark at other dogs, for example, by instinct. Another example of instinct is the be-havior of baby sea turtles, which hatch from their eggs on beaches. Their parents are not there to guide them, but instinct tells the hatch-lings to scurry to the ocean. Once the turtles have reached adulthood, a different instinct draws them back to the same beaches to mate and lay their eggs. Animals acting instinctively do not need to learn.

By the end of the nineteenth century, scientists explained nearly all animal behavior as instinct. Today, however, scientists know that instinct and learning combine in ways that are more complicated than experts used to think.

How Scientists Define Instinct

In the 1960s biologists and psychologists worked on a definition of instinct. They began listing the ways in which instinctual behavior differs from other kinds of behavior. To be considered an instinct, a behavior had to be:

Automatic. The animal does the same thing every time it receives a stimulus, or trigger. The stimulus can be a sensation experienced by the animal, or something that happens around the animal. In the case of a baby monkey, one stimulus is the feeling of motion. This feeling

Instinct leads these newly hatched sea turtles to the water. They won't all survive the trip—instinct also draws predators to the places where turtles hatch.

triggers an automatic, instinctual response—the baby monkey clutches at its mother's hair. Even a newborn monkey has a tight grip, which keeps the infant from falling as its mother moves around on the ground and in trees. The baby monkey does not decide whether or not to grip—gripping is an automatic, instinctual behavior.

Universal. An entire species shares instinctual behavior. All male emperor penguins, for example, balance their eggs on their feet to keep them warm in winter. This doesn't mean that every single member of a given species always obeys instinct. Sometimes one animal does something different, maybe even the opposite of the usual instinctual behavior. For instance, in most species females automatically take care of their young—behavior that is called the maternal, or mothering, instinct. Occasionally the maternal instinct seems to go haywire. A mother animal neglects her young, possibly killing and even eating them. She may be sick or starving. She may have a genetic defect. Or perhaps she knows that something is wrong with her young and they are not likely to survive. In general, though, instinctual behavior is much the same in all the animals of that species.

Not learned. Instinct is **innate**, which means that it is present in an animal from birth. It is not something that the animal learns from its parents or from its own experience. Honeybees are born with the innate ability to build nests out of the wax that their bodies produce. Making nests out of beeswax is instinctual because it is inherited, part of the bees' genetic makeup.

A baby patas monkey clings to its mother as she climbs a tree in Kenya. The mother's movement was a stimulus that triggered the clutching response in her infant.

What about human beings? People are animals. Do they have instincts, too? When Descartes wrote about animal instincts in the seventeenth century, people thought that instinct was much less special and less wonderful than human reason. Later, however, psychologists and other scientists came to see that people have instincts, too—lots of them. Babies are attracted to faces by instinct, for example. People and animals share many instinctive behaviors, such as avoiding fire.

More than Instinct

Instinct explains a lot of animal behavior, but learning is also an important reason for the things animals do. Dogs are not born with an instinct for leading blind people, but some dogs can learn the skills and behaviors they need to guide the blind, such as ignoring other dogs and helping their handlers avoid obstacles.

Dogs can learn to obey commands because the ability to learn is something they have inherited from their wild relatives, wolves and coyotes. These animals usually live in packs led by alphas, or "top dogs." Other pack members, who learn that they are below the alphas in the social order, behave in ways that show respect for the alphas.

Strong bonds often form between dogs and the people with whom they live. Those bonds are built on the same social instincts that bind wild packs together. Because of those instincts, a well-trained domestic dog sees its owner or handler as the leader of its pack. The dog instinctively behaves in ways that will please the leader. But

Guide dogs receive months of training before they are able to safely lead visually impaired people through city streets. What makes that training possible is a dog's instinctive eagerness to bond with the people it is close to.

the dog needs to learn how to recognize its leader. Knowing this, the trainer of a guide dog builds on a foundation of instinct, and this teaching shapes the dog's behavior.

Many other animals act the way they do because of a combination of instinct and learning, but without any training by humans. Songbirds, for example, are born with the instinct to sing, but scientists have found that in many species their songs are not programmed into them at birth. Like human children learning to talk, young songbirds experiment with all kinds of cheeps, peeps, and warbles. Gradually, through trial and error, they learn to imitate their parents' calls and songs.

Beavers are another example of how instinct is shaped by experience. Although beavers are born with the instinctual urge to build dams, they do not always build in the same way. Sometimes beavers don't even bother with dam-building—they move into a pond behind a human-made dam. Or they start with a concrete dam that people have built across a stream and add a layer of logs and mud across its top.

A young beaver echoes its parent's behavior. Born with the dam-building instinct, beavers start arranging sticks while still nursing, but their construction skills improve with practice and experience.

MOKO LEADS THE WAY

In March 2008, two whales were part of a surprising animal rescue in New Zealand. This time whales weren't the rescuers—they were the animals in danger.

Two pygmy sperm whales had run aground at a place called Mahia Beach. The ten-foot-long mother whale and her five-foot-long calf had swum into a narrow channel between the beach and a sandbar, and they could not find their way back to open sea.

Local people, including an employee of the government's Department of Conservation, tried to refloat the stranded whales. Every time the rescuers managed to refloat them, the confused whales once again swam into the sandbar. The animals appeared distressed and were calling to each other with clicks and whistles.

Swimmers at Mahia Beach watch Moko the dolphin twirl a boogie board. Moko not only chose to interact frequently with visitors to the beach but also took action to save the lives of stranded whales.

About thirty whales run aground at Mahia Beach each year. Most cannot be refloated. Wildlife control workers kill them rather than leave them to die slowly. The conservation employee who had tried to save the two pygmy sperm whales was "close to putting them out of their misery," as he later said, when Moko swam to the rescue.

People around Mahia Bay had given the name Moko to a wild dolphin that lived in the area. Friendly and playful, Moko had frolicked with swimmers and kayakers. Never before, though, had she gotten involved in a whale rescue. "Moko just came flying through the water, and pushed in between us and the whales," said one of the rescuers.

The dolphin started clicking and whistling. Were Moko and the whales communicating? It looked that way to witnesses. (All species of dolphins and whales belong to a group of closely related sea mammals called **cetaceans**.) Then Moko swam along the channel between the sandbar and the beach. The whales followed her. At the entrance to an even smaller channel, the dolphin made a sharp right turn, with the whales on her tail. She led them through that narrow channel and out to the open sea. The two whales swam safely away and were not seen in the area again.

The conservation worker reported that Moko probably saved the whales' lives. There have been reports of dolphins saving human swimmers, too. No one knows why dolphins do such things. One possible explanation is that dolphins are "wired" to help other dolphins in distress, and that a dolphin may occasionally mistake a small whale or a human for another dolphin. Or maybe dolphins can feel sympathy for a creature in trouble even if that creature belongs to a different species.

Even when beavers build a complete dam, they have to make a lot of on-the-spot decisions. They must decide how best to use the various kinds and sizes of trees that are available as building materials, and where to place their dams in each lake or stream. The beavers' decisions are based not just on instinct but on everything they have learned since they first helped their parents repair the family dam. All beavers are born with the instinctive ability to build dams, but a beaver that has already built at least one dam can build a new one faster than a beaver that is building its first dam. The dam-building of beavers, like a lot of animal behavior, is a complex mix of instinct and experience.

What About Those Humpback Whales?

Instinct may be the reason the scientists aboard the *Golden Fleece* kept seeing humpback whales save seals from orcas. The particular instinct that might have led the whales to save the seals is shared by many animals. It is called **allomaternalism**, or the allomaternal instinct.

Mothering the Other

When a female animal takes care of her own offspring, she is following the maternal instinct. When she helps or cares for another animal's offspring, scientists say that she is giving allomaternal care (the term means "mothering the other").

Allomaternal care is fairly common in the animal world. Cynthia Moss of the African Wildlife Federation has spent years studying elephants in Africa. She tells the story of a week-old elephant calf in Uganda whose mother had been killed. Two men, a filmmaker and a veterinarian, saw the orphan's plight and decided to introduce it to an elephant family inside a nearby national park. The men took the calf to an elephant herd and let it go, but the young elephant insisted on following its human saviors.

To create a bond between the orphan and the herd, the men pushed the little elephant into a bush, which made the calf trumpet in alarm. When members of the herd trumpeted in reply, the calf heard them and headed in their direction.

The first elephant that the calf approached was a large bull, or male—an unlucky choice. Bull elephants can be impatient with young ones, even their own offspring. The bull swatted the calf with its trunk and knocked it down. Then a cow, or female elephant, reached out to the calf with her trunk. The cow was nursing a calf of her own, but she drew the orphan to her side so that it could nurse as well. By the next day the orphan was part of the elephant family.

Monkeys, apes, and dolphins are also known to provide allomaternal care. Adult females help care for their sisters' offspring, for example, and females may adopt orphaned young animals. In species in which males care for their young, some male animals care for the offspring of others. In one well-known case, two male penguins in a zoo in Bremerhaven, Germany, adopted a penguin egg that had been abandoned by its parents. The males incubated the egg for about a month and then raised the chick that hatched from it.

An adult male Humboldt penguin (with white stripe) grooms the growing chick that it raised, together with another male penguin, in a German zoo. Other male pairs have also raised young penguins from eggs that were abandoned by their biological parents.

Across Species Lines

Allomaternal behavior can cross species lines. When a person adopts a puppy, kitten, or other animal and cares for it, the human is displaying cross-species allomaternalism. When a mother cat lets an orphaned baby squirrel nurse alongside her kittens, or a dog snuggles with a pair of baby rabbits as though they were her puppies, the allomaternal instinct is at work.

An example of allomaternal behavior became a news story around the world in 1996, when a three-year-old boy fell into the gorilla enclosure at a Chicago-area zoo. Instead of attacking the "intruder," a

female gorilla picked him up and gently carried him to the door of the enclosure. Another captive gorilla who became famous for allomaternal behavior was Koko, a female gorilla that cared for several pet cats.

The humpback whales that saved seals from predatory whales might have been feeling allomaternal, too. Even though the whales did not have calves of their own to protect, the sight of a seal being attacked could have triggered the same response as the sight of a whale calf being attacked. The whales protected the seal just as they would have protected their calves. In this way, the whales' life-saving actions can be seen as the result of instinct.

Many of the things people do are the result of instinct, but they also involve emotions. The urge to find a mate, for example, is an instinct—one that leads to love songs, heartbreak, and joy. Instinct drives parents to care for their newborn baby, but the bond they feel with the baby produces a surge of powerful emotions. Even if the humpback whales acted on instinct when they saved seals from predators, could the whales have had feelings about the situation, too? "When a human protects an imperiled individual of another species, we call it compassion," say scientists who were aboard the *Golden Fleece*. "If a humpback whale does so, we call it instinct. But sometimes the distinction isn't all that clear."

The question of whether animals have emotions is an old one. Scientists are now searching for the answer in animal behavior—and also deep inside the brains of animals and human beings.

The urge to care for creatures of other species is not limited to human beings. Koko the gorilla is one of several captive primates that have had pet cats.

2. DO ANIMALS HAVE EMOTIONS?

Enormous humpback whales are not the only creatures that make us wonder whether animals have emotions. Even the smallest creatures can surprise us with behavior we do not understand.

Two baby mice became trapped overnight in a garage sink. They could not climb up the slippery sides to escape. By the time the owner of the house found the mice, they appeared tired and scared. What happened next was "a small act of heroism," in the words of Marc Bekoff, an ethologist and **biology** professor who has studied animal behavior for years. It might also have been an act of **empathy**, which is recognizing the needs and feelings of others.

The homeowner put a small dish of water and some bits of food in the sink. One mouse hopped to the water and drank, but the other mouse seemed too weak to move. Then the stronger mouse found a piece of food and carried it to the weaker mouse, who nibbled at it. While the weaker mouse nibbled, the stronger mouse moved the food a little at a time until it was close to the water dish. The weaker mouse

If one mouse helps another, does that mean these creatures feel emotions such as fear or pity? Many scientists suspect that animals' emotional lives are more complex—and maybe more like our own—than we think.

followed the food. Eventually the mouse reached the water and was able to drink. The homeowner put a piece of wood in the sink to serve as a ramp. Once the food and water had restored their strength, the mice made their way up the ramp and escaped from the sink.

"What happened in the sink?" Bekoff asks in *Wild Justice*, a book he wrote with philosopher Jessica Pierce. "Did one mouse actually understand that the other mouse was in trouble and find a way to help? Did the tiny creature display a kind of empathy?" Most scientists would warn against reading human-sounding emotions into the mouse's actions. They would be on guard against anthropomorphism. "Yet it is also possible," say Bekoff and Pierce, "to read too little into the animals we watch. Perhaps mice have the capacity to feel sorry for another mouse in distress, and to offer help."

The story of the mice in the sink is an **anecdote**, meaning that it is someone's account of an event. To scientists, anecdotes make poor evidence. It is often impossible, or at least very difficult, to prove that an anecdote is true. And even when an example of unusual animal behavior—for example, whales rescuing a seal—is reported by reliable witnesses and captured on film, it is still a single, isolated event.

In 2011 people at an Idaho zoo noticed a large elk known as Shooter pawing at the water in his large water tank. Witnesses finally saw Shooter put his head into the tank. When the elk raised his head, he was carrying a small marmot—a member of the rodent family—in his jaws. The marmot had apparently fallen into the tank and was in danger of drowning. Shooter placed it on the ground and nudged it gently with his hoof until it recovered and scampered away.

"[Shooter] deliberately took that animal out of the tank," reported a zoo employee. A witness with a video camera had captured the entire rescue. Still, scientists cannot say exactly what this unusual example of animal behavior meant. It was a single, isolated event.

Scientists are cautious about basing new ideas on single events. But if anecdotes about a certain kind of animal behavior seem convincing, or if the stories keep piling up, scientists may start looking for more examples of the behavior. They may even be able to design an experiment to test it. Even though anecdotal evidence is not strong enough to prove a scientific point, it can lead to new research.

Animals Act Emotional

People who spend a lot of time around animals see many things that look like evidence of feelings and emotional reactions. Pet owners, veterinarians, animal trainers, and others have reported thousands of case studies suggesting that animals' lives are full of emotion.

Even in humans, emotions are difficult to study, because not everyone experiences feelings in the same way. With animals the challenge is greater because scientists cannot communicate with animals or know for certain what they feel. Still, a lot of scientifically trained observers have told of animal behavior that would be recognized as emotional if people did it.

Birds: The Feathered Fury of Ravens

Bernd Heinrich is a biologist who has spent years studying ravens, large birds that belong to the same family as crows. "Anger is not confined

to humans," says Heinrich, who has seen ravens display this powerful feeling. The strongest show of anger was aimed at Heinrich himself, on a day when he climbed up to a ravens' nest to handle their young.

The first sign of anger from the parent birds was a series of high-pitched alarm calls as Heinrich approached. When these calls failed to drive him away, the ravens' cries grew longer and took on a snarling, growling sound. The ravens also hopped up and down on branches with their feathers puffed out, a behavior that was probably meant to make the birds look larger and more threatening.

Finally, when Heinrich started handling one of the young ravens in the nest, the parents exploded with anger. They flew close to his head, gave loud rasping calls, pounded on branches with their beaks, and ripped twigs from nearby branches and threw them at him.

"Fear, anger, love, hate, and curiosity" drive much raven behavior, says Heinrich. Ravens' behavior may also be driven by automatic instinct and intelligent problem-solving, he points out, but emotion is definitely part of the picture.

Primates: Brother-Sister Competition

Bonobos, once called pygmy chimpanzees, are **primates**, members of the animal group that includes apes and humans. Along with chim-panzees and gorillas, bonobos have been studied by scientists who want to find out whether apes can learn to communicate with peo-ple. As **primatologist** Sue Savage-Rumbaugh worked with a bonobo named Kanzi and his sister Panbanisha, she learned that bonobos can sulk and feel jealous of their siblings, just as people can.

"Fear, anger, love, hate, and curiosity" are part of what makes ravens tick, says Bernd Heinrich, a scientist who has studied these large, intelligent birds.

Kanzi the bonobo communicates with his trainer, Sue Savage-Rumbaugh, using symbols called lexigrams. Kanzi's actions revealed that he sometimes felt jealous, angry, embarrassed, or hungry for attention.

Kanzi became something of a primate superstar. He could solve puzzles on a computer, make stone tools, and draw pictures. He understood the meanings of many lexigrams, which are symbols that stand for words in a language invented for primate experiments. Photographers and film crews showed up to capture images of Kanzi, and he enjoyed the attention. But when photographers from the *London Times* took pictures of Panbanisha instead of Kanzi, he was so upset that he destroyed his electronic keyboard.

Panbanisha's successes angered Kanzi. When she made a stone tool, he charged at her. When she drew lexigrams on the floor that were better than his own, he threw her crayons around. When Savage-Rumbaugh gave the bonobos an electric guitar, Panbanisha played better than Kanzi—and when it was time to play the guitar again, Kanzi became threatening. When Kanzi tried to drive Panbanisha out of the room, the scientist took Panbanisha outside, leaving Kanzi to sulk. He screamed, then ripped the arms from a toy panda.

Afterward, Kanzi tried to put the arms back on the stuffed toy, and when he couldn't do that, he carried the toy and the arms around the room. Head down, eyes turned away from everyone, Kanzi seemed to feel sorry for, or ashamed of, his behavior.

Elephants: Love and Grief

A baby elephant is a very big deal. A female elephant normally bears just one calf every four or five years. She gestates her young, or carries it inside her, for almost two years before giving birth, and she nurses it for another four years or even longer. With so much time and energy invested in each calf, it makes sense for elephants to have a strong maternal instinct. Wildlife researchers who have observed these mighty mammals in the wild say that sometimes their instinct cannot be separated from emotion.

In 1990 wildlife researcher Cynthia Moss saw a moving example of maternal care in a herd of wild elephants in Kenya. A senior female named Echo had given birth to a calf, but the baby elephant was unable to stand and walk. Something seemed to be wrong with the joints

in his front legs—he could not straighten them. The newborn calf was exhausted from trying to move. The herd had moved away, except for Echo and her daughter Enid. Both females tried to raise the calf to his feet with their trunks, but failed.

Slowly, with the tired calf shuffling on his front knees, the three moved to a nearby mudhole, where Echo and Enid splashed the calf with water to protect him from the heat. At this point all the little elephant could do was scream. Enid started off after the herd, but her brother's cries of distress drew her back to his side. Echo never left the calf. Unable to stand, the calf could barely nurse. Moss feared that he would not last the night.

The following morning the calf was still alive. For two days his mother and sister helped him shuffle along very slowly on his bent front legs. Although they had fallen far behind their herd, Echo and Enid did not abandon the calf. Finally the joints in the calf's legs began to work properly, and on the third day he managed to stand up at last. Moss gave the calf the name Ely. He survived to adulthood.

Tonie, a young female elephant observed by researcher Joyce Poole, was not as lucky as Echo. Tonie's calf was born dead. For a day Tonie tried to bring the calf to life, raising his body repeatedly with her trunk. Then, for two days, she stood by his body. Her head, ears, and trunk hung limp, the corners of her mouth sagged down, and she barely moved. To Poole, it was clear that Tonie's face and body expressed grief.

An elephant called Tonie stands over the body of her calf, which was born dead. Tonie tried again and again to raise the calf, then remained by its side for several days. Her behavior may have been shaped by instinct, but it also showed all the signs of grief.

Echo and Tonie had instinctively bonded with their young. But Moss questions whether instinct was the only force behind their behavior:

> Elephants eat when they feel hungry, drink when they feel thirsty, run when they feel frightened, scream when they feel pain. Is it such a leap to say that as an elephant gently touches her calf with her trunk, she feels love?

Reptiles: Cold-Blooded, With Feeling

Whales, dolphins, primates, and elephants have something in common with humans. They are mammals. This means that they are warm-blooded (their bodies produce heat to maintain a steady temperature), they give birth to live young, and they nurse their young with milk from mammary glands. Most pets and farm animals, such as dogs, cats, cattle, sheep, and horses, are also mammals. Birds are not mammals—they lay eggs and do not nurse their young—but they are warm-blooded, too.

Because these animals are like us in some ways, it may be easy for us to think that they have feelings similar to our own. After all, animals sometimes do things that seem a lot like the ways we express emotion. Chimpanzees grin, for example. Dogs jump with excitement. We can interpret these actions as emotional, even when we aren't sure exactly what emotions the animals are feeling. But what about creatures that are less closely related to us, such as lizards and turtles? Is there any way to know if they have feelings?

The temperatures of reptiles—such as this European pond turtle being measured by Italian scientists—sometimes rise when the animals are handled. This may mean that cold-blooded creatures have emotions.

Lizards and turtles are reptiles, cold-blooded animals whose body temperature depends on their environment. A reptile controls its body temperature by moving toward or away from sources of heat and cold, such as sunlight, warm rocks, or shadows. Reptiles seek heat when they are suffering from a fever, which is an increase in body temperature because of an illness or physical condition. This heat-seeking behavior, together with a discovery about laboratory rats, may have given scientists a clue to reptiles' inner lives.

In the 1970s scientists discovered that the body temperatures of laboratory rats rose after the rats were handled. The higher temperature seemed to be a sign of alarm or distress, even if the handling was gentle and friendly. If the same person handled a rat over time, the rat got used to that person, and its temperature no longer went up when it was handled. Then, if a new person handled the rat, the rat's temperature went up again.

Scientists decided that the rise in temperature must be caused by the animals' mental or emotional reactions, not by simple physical reactions. A physical reaction would be instinctual or automatic. It would not change when the rat became more comfortable or less comfortable.

Emotional fever is the scientific term for a rise in body temperature with no physical cause. It happens in humans, too. In one experiment, for example, students' core body temperatures went up a little before a test. Scientists have found that many species of mammals and birds show emotional fever when they are under stress. The animal's heart rate often speeds up slightly as its temperature rises.

Reptiles may be cold-blooded, but they may show signs of emotional fever. Scientists have measured higher temperatures and heart rates in lizards, turtles, and snakes after gentle handling. When the handlers release the reptiles, the animals move toward heat sources, just as if they had fevers—but with no disease or other physical reason for a fever. Some researchers think that the reptiles may be experiencing emotional fever, as rats and other mammals do. If so, emotional fever may mean that the reptiles have feelings of some kind, even if they are as basic as discomfort and comfort.

No Fever, No Feelings?

Fish are cold-blooded, like reptiles, but they do not show emotional fever. Michel Cabanac, a scientist who studies how living things control their body temperatures, has suggested that because fish lack emotional fever, they may be "mostly like robots." Other experts are not so sure. Emotional fever is just one sign of inner awareness and feelings. There may be others.

Researchers are exploring ways to test fish for feelings. One key question is whether fish feel pain. It is a hard question to answer.

Pain is complicated. Scientists are still discovering how humans experience it, but there are several steps in the process. First, cells somewhere in the body react to damage, injury, or illness—a stubbed toe, for example. These cells send nerve signals to the brain, which creates the sensation of pain, and the toe-stubber yells, "Ow, my toe!"

Pain normally has two parts: the physical source of pain, and the mental awareness of pain. Certain kinds of damage to a person's brain or nervous system can interfere with this pain mechanism. If the mechanism is not working normally, a person can suffer an injury—cutting his foot on a piece of broken glass, say, or burning her hand on a hot stove—and not feel pain, or even know that the damage has happened. Or a person can suffer severe, long-lasting pain with no definite physical cause that doctors can find.

Putting the Heat to Goldfish

To test fish for pain sensitivity, researchers must try to cause temporary pain to the fish—something that researchers do only because they want to learn whether fish can feel pain, which might lead to better overall treatment of fish. In a 2009 experiment involving goldfish, researchers attached small foil heaters to the fish. By gradually raising the temperature of the heaters, the researchers could cause discomfort or pain without damaging the fish.

Before the experiment started, all the fish received shots. Half the fish were injected with morphine, a powerful painkiller. The other half were injected with a fluid that had no effect on pain.

The experimenters thought that the fluid-treated fish would show signs of pain before the morphine-treated ones. Instead, all of the fish reacted to the heat at the same time, by wriggling. As soon as the fish showed distress by wriggling, the researchers turned the heaters off.

After the experiment, the fish that had received morphine behaved the same way as before they received the shot. They appeared

"Fish don't feel pain" has been repeated thousands of times, but is it true? Research on goldfish suggests that fish may experience and remember painful sensations.

normally relaxed, swimming around without wriggling. But the fish that had not gotten morphine were defensive. Instead of swimming around, they "hovered," or moved as little as possible. Scientists think that hovering in a fish is a sign of anxiety, fear, or caution. The two groups of fish—one that had received a painkiller and one that had not—acted differently after the experiment with the heaters. What did this mean?

Wriggling when something strange happens to its body might be a fish's reflex—an automatic, instinctive reaction. (An example of a human reflex is the way a person's foot kicks up when a doctor taps the knee with a small, rubber hammer.) Many people, including some scientists, think that when a fish struggles on a hook or flops wildly after being taken from the water, the fish's behavior is a reflex, without the sensation of pain as we know it.

When the heaters were turned on, all of the goldfish wriggled, which may have been a reflex. But the researchers think that the goldfishes' behavior after the experiment means that fish *do* feel pain. The goldfish that got morphine acted normal because they had not felt pain—or if they did feel it, they did not remember it. The other fish felt pain, remembered it, and acted differently because of it. Morphine changed the way the fish experienced the heat, although scientists do not yet know how the drug's effects on fish compare to its effects on humans and other mammals.

Scientists are a long way from knowing for certain that fish feel pain, or anything else. But in her 2010 book titled *Do Fish Feel Pain?* zoologist Victoria Braithwaite of Pennsylvania State University points

JENNY THE ORANGUTAN AND WILLY DARWIN

Today Charles Darwin is remembered mostly for explaining how new species of plants and animals evolve, or develop, from existing species. His 1859 book *On the Origin of Species* laid the foundation for evolutionary biology, the branch of science that studies how the many forms of life are related. In the course of his life Darwin (1809–1882) investigated many subjects, including emotion in animals and people. He first researched emotion with the help of two "assistants," one ape, one human.

In 1838, at a London zoo, Darwin saw his first ape—an orangutan called Jenny from Southeast Asia. He wrote that when the keeper would not give Jenny an apple, "she threw herself on her back, kicked & cried, precisely like a naughty child." When the keeper gave Jenny the fruit, Darwin reported, she looked "contented." Later Darwin climbed into the cage with the orangutan to observe her more closely. At different times he noted that her facial expressions seemed bashful, pouting, or puzzled.

Charles Darwin got the world's attention by showing that apes and humans are descended from the same distant ancestors. He was one of the first scientists to record emotional behavior in apes and other mammals—including his own children.

The next year Darwin's wife gave birth to their first child, a boy whom they named William. Fascinated with the baby's movements and expressions, Darwin sat beside Willy's cot, observing his offspring and recording the baby's first signs of anger, fear, and pleasure. When Darwin showed Willy a mirror for the first time, the scientist compared his son's reaction to that of Jenny the orangutan.

In 1872 Darwin wrote about these and many other observations in a book called *The Expression of the Emotions in Man and Animals*. Darwin had no doubt that animals, like people, "feel pleasure and pain, happiness, and misery." As part of the animal world, Darwin reasoned, humans share many physical features with other animals. Why wouldn't they share some emotional qualities as well?

to growing evidence that fishes' memories, mental activities, and sensations are more complicated than experts used to think.

It's In the Brain

The more scientists learn about how human emotions work, the more tools they have for studying emotions in animals. Some of the most powerful tools come from **neuroscience**, the branch of science that studies the workings of the brain, the nervous system, and the chemicals that flow through and around the brain.

Neuroscientists and biologists have discovered that certain parts of the human brain are closely tied to the emotions we feel. Brain chemicals are also related to human emotions. Some of the brain features and chemicals that shape our feelings are shared by animals. Scientists do not yet know whether this means that animals share our ability to feel emotions as well, but the possibility exists.

The Amygdala

In the nineteenth century scientists identified a small, almond-shaped region in the human brain that they called the amygdala. There are two amygdalas in the brain, one on each side. They receive messages, or stimuli, from the senses—especially from the sense of smell. These messages cause the amygdalas to release chemicals called hormones and neurotransmitters, which change the brain's chemistry. Changes in brain chemistry have a big impact on mental processes such as memory and emotion.

During the twentieth century, neuroscientists studied people with damaged amygdalas. They also experimented on animals by

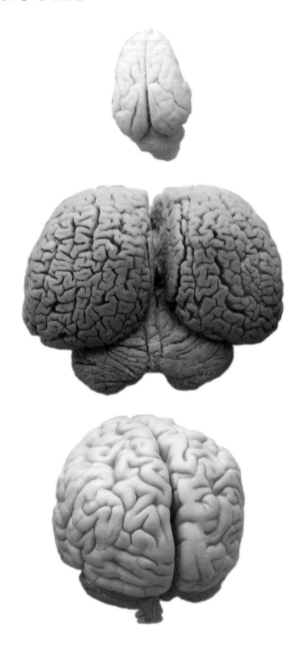

The brains of (top to bottom) a wild pig, a bottlenose dolphin, and a human differ in size but are all divided into left and right sections, or hemispheres. These brains and those of many other species share another feature, the amygdalas—small regions linked to powerful emotional states such as aggression.

operating on their amygdalas. These researchers discovered that people and animals with damaged amygdalas do not show fear and other emotions in the normal ways. Their social interactions were abnormal, too—they could not recognize facial expressions, for example. Other research has proved that when people are frightened, there is a lot of activity in their amygdalas.

Studies of the amygdala continue today. This brain region seems to be connected with emotional states such as fear, aggression, anxiety, maternal care, and empathy. It may help create what neuroscientists call "emotional memory," the strong positive and negative feelings that leave lasting impressions.

Mammals, reptiles, birds, and amphibians all have amygdalas. But animals' brains are not miniature human brains—they are structured differently in many ways. Now some animal researchers hope to discover what role the amygdala plays in the mental lives of different species. This small part of the brain may be key to understanding how animals experience feelings such as fear.

Spindle and Mirror Neurons

The cells that make up the nervous system are called neurons, or nerve cells. There are various kinds of neurons. Two types, spindle neurons and mirror neurons, are especially important to emotional activity in humans, and perhaps in animals as well.

Spindle neurons, also called Von Economo neurons or VENs, were first identified in the human brain. They are much larger than other brain cells, and they move information in the form of electrical charges across the brain faster than other cells. Spindle neurons are found in parts of human brains that are active during speech, social interaction, and strong feelings such as love and suffering.

Neuroscientists were not surprised when, in 1999, spindle neurons were found in the brains of the great apes—chimpanzees, gorillas, and orangutans. These primates are humans' closest relatives. Then, in 2006, researchers found spindle neurons in orcas, humpback whales, and several other kinds of whales. Since then researchers have identified spindle cells in the brains of additional whale and dolphin species, and most recently in elephants. These special neurons may have evolved to carry electrical signals rapidly across big brains.

Mirror neurons were discovered in the 1990s by Italian researchers who had placed implants in monkeys' brains. The researchers' goal was to study the animals' brain activity during various activities. They discovered that certain brain cells fired, or showed electrical activity, when the monkeys picked up food.

At lunchtime one of the researchers happened to reach for his food and saw a monkey watching him. To the researcher's surprise, the monkey's brain cells fired in the same way as when the monkey itself picked up food. Further research showed that some brain cells, which became known as mirror neurons, are activated whether a monkey performs an action or sees another monkey (or a person) perform the action.

Mirror neurons appear to exist in humans, primates, and possibly songbirds. Scientists are still debating exactly what mirror neurons are and how they work. Some researchers, though, think that these cells may be vital to language skills. Language is learned by imitation, as when young songbirds imitate the songs of their parents. Mirror neurons may help with this because they are a built-in form of mimicry, or imitation.

Some scientists think that mirror neurons are also involved in empathy. These cells may help us understand other people because, at a very basic level, we feel what they are feeling.

Hormones and Emotions

Brain chemicals are another feature that humans share with animals. Our bodies produce chemicals that affect our moods and emotions. For example, oxytocin, nicknamed the "cuddle chemical," is a hormone linked to feelings of love and attachment. All mammals have it. Dopamine is a neurotransmitter related to the brain's pleasure center. Activities such as eating and mating release dopamine, which is found in a vast variety of animals, including worms. A different neurotransmitter, serotonin, helps balance mood, appetite, and sleep. It is also found in most animals, from worms to humans.

When the balance of hormones or neurotransmitters changes, people experience emotions ranging from joy to depression. Do these chemicals have the same effect on animals? Experiments have found that lobsters with unusually high or low levels of serotonin are more aggressive than normal. Drugs that change people's emotional states also work on animals. If a pet cat or dog has a behavior problem, such as destroying furniture or howling when its human companion is away, a veterinarian may treat the animal with one of

Two spiny lobsters confronting each other over territory may have more or less serotonin than the average lobster. Unusual levels of this chemical, which is also found in human brains, make these sea creatures especially aggressive.

the same antidepressant drugs that doctors use to treat anxiety or sadness in their human patients—and get the same results.

Humans are related through evolution to all other animals. It makes sense that some features of human brains are found in animals' brains, too. If these features are strongly linked to feelings in people, maybe the same is true in animals.

3. THE GROUP AND THE SELF

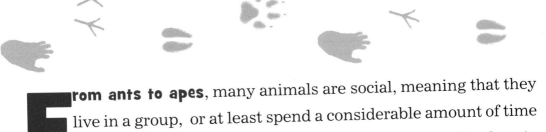

From ants to apes, many animals are social, meaning that they live in a group, or at least spend a considerable amount of time around others of their kind. Some researchers look for clues to animal emotion in the way social animals behave toward each other. Others try to answer one of the biggest questions of animal research: Do animals have selfhood—a sense of their own identities?

When Helping Is Selfish

One lively area of research in animal behavior concerns **altruism**, which means doing something that is good for someone else. An altruistic act helps another, but it costs the helper something. People who donate to charity or do volunteer work, for example, are altruistic. They give their own resources—money or time—to be used by others.

Altruism is common among animals, too, especially in species that have complex social organizations. In animal altruism, one animal gives food to another, uses its energy to help another, or risks its own

Ants are social insects that live in large colonies and communicate by scent and with taps of their feet and antennae. Ant society is based on cooperation—but will one ant risk its life to rescue another? Researchers designed an experiment to find out.

safety to warn others of danger. In other words, an altruistic animal "spends" resources on others instead of itself. Biologists call the altruistic animal the donor. The one that gets the help is the recipient.

When a human donor is altruistic, he or she has made a conscious decision to help someone else, even if it means self-sacrifice. What reasons might animals have for helping others? Altruistic actions take something away from the donor's strength or chances of survival, but the driving force behind evolution is survival—so why would altruism evolve in the animal world? To answer these questions, sociobiologists have studied the behavior of social animals such as ants and monkeys. They have found several explanations for altruism.

Insects: Ants and Altruism

Many insights into animal altruism come from the study of social insects such as ants, bees, and wasps, which live in colonies or nests that contain many individuals. The social lives of these insects are built around sacrifice and altruism.

Members of an ant colony share food, defend their queen, and care for her offspring. To achieve their social organization, the insects have even sacrificed their ability to reproduce—the queen is the only one who breeds and bears young. But would an ant risk its life to save another ant's life? Four scientists designed an experiment to find out.

Animals sometimes rescue other animals from danger, but these rescues are "extremely rare," say the scientists who created the ant experiment. They tested a Mediterranean ant species *Cataglyphis cursor* to see whether ants would rescue another ant trapped under loose sand, a common peril of ant life. This time, though, the ant was trapped by more than sand. A fine nylon line around one leg held it firmly in place.

The scientists watched how free-roaming ants treated a series of trapped ants. If the trapped ant was from the same nest as the free ants, the free ants tried to rescue it. They dug sand away from it, pulled on its legs, and bit the nylon line—even though they risked being trapped under shifting sand along with the victim. But if the trapped ant was from a different species, or from the same species but a different nest, the free ants did not try to help it.

The ants' rescue behavior showed two things. First, the ants showed problem-solving skills when they came face-to-face with an unfamiliar danger, the nylon thread. They tried to bite it. Second, the ants' altruism was directed only at relatives. (Because all of the ants in a nest are born from the same queen, all nestmates are related to each other.) The ants were willing to risk danger to try to rescue another ant, but only if the trapped ant shared their genetic makeup.

The behavior of the rescuing ants was most likely instinct, shaped over millions of years by a force that scientists call kin selection or kin-specific altruism.

Kin Selection

Kin selection is one explanation for acts of animal altruism. It means that if the donor and the recipient are related, the donor benefits by helping the recipient, because they share a genetic heritage. If the donor's help makes it possible for the recipient to survive and reproduce, the recipient will pass on its genes to its offspring. The donor shares some of the recipient's genes, so the donor's heritage will be passed along, too.

Parental care is a kind of kin selection. Parents care for and protect their offspring because the offspring will carry the parents' genetic heritage into future generations.

Remember the story of the two baby mice trapped in the sink? If the two mice were siblings—which seems likely—kin selection might help explain why the stronger mouse became a donor, helping the weaker one. The cost to the donor mouse was not great. By sharing the food and water, and by using a little energy to move the piece of food, the donor made it possible for both mice to survive. This doubled the chances that some of the donor's genetic material would be reproduced in the next generation of mice.

Animal altruism is generally stronger in close relationships than distant ones. In the case of Belding's ground squirrels, small rodents of the American West, researchers found that female squirrels show more altruism toward full siblings (donor and recipient have the same mother and father) than half-siblings (donor and recipient have the same mother but different fathers). A study of Japanese macaque monkeys revealed that the monkeys make bigger sacrifices for offspring than for nephews and nieces, and bigger sacrifices for siblings than for cousins.

A female Belding's ground squirrel and her young survey their territory. Females sometimes share food and nest space with each other. They are more generous toward close relatives than toward more distant ones.

Kin selection is not limited to mammals. Among African birds called pied kingfishers, males without mates often become "helpers" to mated pairs, guarding their nests and bringing them food. These altruistic males, however, are much more likely to help their relatives than to help birds that are not related to them.

Reciprocity: Vampires Share Blood

Kin selection is not the only reason for animal altruism. Animals sometimes do things that benefit unrelated animals, or even animals of other species, at some cost or risk to themselves. One possible explanation for this behavior is reciprocity, or an exchange of benefits—"I'll help you now, but I expect you to help me if I need help in the future." This type of altruism is not yet fully understood. Experts disagree about how to define it and study it.

Vampire bats have been studied as an example of reciprocal altruism. These bats roost in large social groups by day. By night they feed on blood from living mammals such as cattle—and, on rare occasions, people. If a vampire bat goes for two nights without feeding, it is likely to die. On any given night, however, not all bats will succeed in finding a meal. To prevent starvation in the colony, vampire bats that have fed will share the food by regurgitating (throwing up) blood into hungry bats' mouths.

The sharing of blood among colony members looks like reciprocity, but some scientists question whether this behavior is truly reciprocal. For one thing, colony members are often siblings, cousins, nieces, or nephews of other colony members, so kin selection may be involved.

Vampire bats feed on blood from living mammals such as cattle. A bat that has fed successfully may share the blood with one that has not found food.

Within each colony, some subgroups of bats spend more time with each other than with others, and food sharing seems to happen most often among members of these close groups—which are also often related.

Another question concerns "freeloaders." In the view of some scientists, true reciprocity means that animals can keep track of who has helped and who has been helped. An individual that refuses to help others will not receive help when it is in need, or the system would break down under the strain of takers who never give back. So far, researchers have not found that blood-sharing among vampire bats meets this strict standard of reciprocity.

Even if kin selection and reciprocity account for altruistic behavior in animals, questions remain to be investigated. Is altruism always automatic and instinctive? Are all members of a species equally altruistic (or non-altruistic)? Are there some acts of altruism that cannot be explained by kin selection or reciprocity? Finally, is it possible that animals that give or receive help from others feel something like generosity or gratitude, even though their behavior is driven by instinct and evolution?

Baboons: Social Stress

Living in groups has a lot of benefits for social animals. Group members can help each other find food, fight off predators, and care for or protect their young. They can also give each other something that many human animals know all too well: stress.

Robert Sapolsky is a neuroscientist who has studied stress in baboons for many years. These African monkeys live in troops ranging in size from 20 to as many as 250 individuals. Baboons' social groups have strict hierarchies, or levels of rank. High-ranking, or dominant, animals have much more power than low-ranking, subordinate ones.

Baboon behavior has a lot to do with an individual's place in the hierarchy. Baboons spend time and energy showing obedience and respect to higher-ranking animals and threatening or bullying lower-ranking ones. In the course of all this social interaction, baboons can be aggressive toward each other. Some disagreements blow up into serious fights.

Social maneuvering takes its toll. Sapolsky and his fellow researchers found that many unhealthy baboons have high levels of stress hormones. These animals appear to live with ongoing psycho-

Three very young baboons squabble with a juvenile, or immature, member of their troop. Stand-offs, displays of aggression, and confrontations are part of daily life for these primates, some of which have stress-related illnesses.

logical and social stress, which floods their brains and bodies with the stress hormones. Over time, their immune systems and even their reproductive systems stop working normally. Among both male and female baboons, low-ranking animals have more stress than high-ranking ones. However, a 2011 study showed that the highest-ranking baboons suffer from stress, too. It's not easy staying on top.

In humans, the physical signs of stress often come with emotional symptoms, such as anxiety, depression, or fear. It's not yet clear whether other primates also "feel" stress in the same ways.

ANIMAL RIGHTS AND WRONGS

Research into animals' feelings and thoughts is controversial because it raises questions about how we should treat animals. For example, studies of **cognition**, or thinking, in dolphins suggest that these cetaceans may be the second-most-intelligent creatures on the planet, after humans. Psychologist Diana Reiss and cetacean expert Lori Marino argue that dolphins, because of their intelligence, should be considered "non-human persons," freed from performing in amusement parks, and given stronger legal protection from being killed for food or by accident.

Science cannot yet give clear, definite answers to many questions about animals' intelligence or their emotions. Nearly all experts, however, agree that at least some animals have **sentience**—that is, they have awareness and are capable of basic feelings such as pain, fear, and comfort. Some scientists limit sentience to mammals, or to mammals and birds. Others include reptiles and fish. Irish researcher Robert Elwood has found evidence that lobsters and crabs feel pain, which would mean that they are sentient creatures, too.

The concept of sentience is the basis for laws in many countries against cruelty to animals. The idea behind such laws is that even though humans use animals for their own purposes—as beasts of burden and as food, for example—people have a duty to treat animals humanely, or decently, and to spare them unnecessary suffering. Based on recent research into pain awareness, some animal researchers say that anti-cruelty laws should be expanded to include a wider range of living things.

Animal cruelty laws vary from place to place. In the United States, federal laws govern the slaughter of livestock, and individual states have laws that cover the treatment of pets, farm animals, and wildlife. Non-governmental organizations such as the American Society for the Prevention of Cruelty to Animals (ASPCA) and the Humane Society of the United States have three goals: to provide care and adoption services for animals in need of help, to promote the enforcement of animal cruelty laws, and to educate the public about animal treatment.

Dolphins that perform in amusement parks seem to be enjoying themselves, and maybe they are. The question, though, is whether humans have the right to hold these intelligent animals captive.

The Animal in the Mirror

Human beings have a sense of selfhood. This means that they are aware of their own existence in the world, and they recognize themselves. One sign of self-awareness is called mirror self-recognition, which means knowing that the face you see in a mirror is yourself, not someone else. Psychologists say that children start recognizing themselves in mirrors as early as eighteen months of age.

Humans were once thought to be the only species capable of mirror self-recognition. All animals were believed to react to mirrors just as babies do—by treating them like other animals. Then, in 1970, a psychologist named Gordon Gallup Jr. invented a simple mirror self-recognition (MSR) test for chimpanzees.

Gallup marked chimpanzees with spots of dye. When the chimpanzees looked in the mirror, their behavior went through four stages. First they acted as though their reflections were other chimpanzees. Then they examined the mirror and looked behind it, as if searching for that "other" animal. In the third stage, the animals made movements in front of the mirror. They appeared to be testing to see if the image in the mirror moved when they did.

By the fourth stage, the chimpanzees clearly recognized that the reflections were of their own bodies. While looking at the mirror, they touched the dye spots on their bodies, and they turned and moved their bodies to see the spots more clearly in the mirror. This showed that a chimpanzee can understand that a mirror image is a reflection of itself.

Animals usually view their reflections as other animals, such as the "enemy" that this golden weaver attacks in the mirror. A few species, however, recognize their reflections as images of themselves—a self-awareness that they share with human beings.

Since that time, other animals have "passed" the MSR test. Individual bonobos, orangutans, and several species of monkeys recognize themselves in mirrors. They even use mirrors to see parts of their bodies that they can't usually see, such as the insides of their mouths. Wild gorillas ignore mirrors, possibly because these animals avoid eye contact with each other—it is a sign of aggression. However, several captive gorillas that are used to socializing with humans have passed the MSR test.

Non-primates have passed the test, too. In 2001 researchers using large mirrors and tanks succeeded in testing orcas and bottlenose dolphins, who passed. Similar results were reported for elephants in 2006. These animals, like humans and apes, are fairly large-brained. However, in 2008 researchers reported that magpies, birds about the size of crows, showed mirror self-recognition, and there have been some claims for pigeons as well.

A human's sense of selfhood goes beyond the ability to recognize his or her reflection in a mirror. It includes memories, relationships with the world and with other people, thoughts, and feelings. Yet mirror self-recognition is known to be just one step in the development of full self-awareness—a step that is also taken by some of our fellow animals.

All animal life on Earth is interrelated. Still, each kind of animal, from the smallest beetle to the largest blue whale, followed its own evolutionary path to its present form. Each species has needs, instincts, and senses that are not exactly like those of any other species.

Whatever animals' feelings may be like, we can be sure that they are not exactly like ours—but that does not mean they are not worth our interest.

Human beings have learned to understand and respect the great diversity of living things in all shapes and sizes. We may discover that the world of animal emotions is equally rich and diverse.

GLOSSARY

allomaternalism   When an animal adopts or cares for a young animal that
                        is not its own offspring; the two animals are usually, but
                        not always, the same species.

altruism   Doing good or helping another at some cost to oneself.

anecdote   Based on an informal account of what happened; not strong
                        scientific evidence because it has not been tested.

anthropomorphism   Thinking that animals' features, characteristics, and re
                        actions are like those of humans; interpreting animals in
                        human terms.

biology   Scientific study of living things.

cetacean   Member of the group of sea mammals that includes
                        whales, dolphins, and porpoises.

cognition   Mental activity; the act of thinking.

emotional fever   A rise in an animal's core body temperature that is due to
                        psychological or mental causes rather than physical causes.

empathy   Recognizing the needs and feelings of others.

ethology   Scientific study of animal behavior.

evolution	Process by which new species develop over time because of changes, or mutations, in existing species.
innate	Present from birth; inborn.
instinct	Pattern of behavior that is genetically programmed, and that all members of a species are born with.
intelligence	Ability to learn, reason, apply knowledge, and interact with others and with the world.
neuroscience	Branch of science that studies the structure and workings of the brain and nervous system.
predator	Animal that preys on, or hunts and eats, other animals.
prey	Animal that is hunted or killed by a predator.
primates	Group of animals that includes monkeys, apes, and humans.
primatologist	Scientist who studies primates.
psychology	Study of the mind; comparative psychologists study the differences and similarities between human and animal minds.
sentience	Awareness of sensations (from sense organs); consciousness; has to do with sensations or feelings, not with thinking.
sociobiologist	Scientist who studies how animals that live in social groups —such as ants and zebras—interact with each other.
species	Group of plants or animals that are enough like one another to have offspring that are able to produce offspring of their own.
zoology	Branch of biology that studies animals, including insects.

FIND OUT MORE

Books

Bekoff, Marc, ed. *The Smile of a Dolphin: Remarkable Accounts of Animal Emotions*. New York: Discovery Books, 2000.

Boysen, Sally. *The Smartest Animals on the Planet*. Buffalo, NY: Firefly, 2009.

Hearne, Vicki. *Animal Happiness: A Moving Exploration of Animals and Their Emotions*. New York: Skyhorse, 2007.

Page, George. *Inside the Animal Mind: A Groundbreaking Exploration of Animal Intelligence*. New York: Broadway, 2001.

Ryan, Marla Felkins. *The Planet's Most Extreme Thinkers*. Farmington Hills, MI: Blackbirch, 2004.

Websites

Animal Emotions

www.psychologytoday.com/blog/animal-emotions

The website of *Psychology Today* includes this blog by Marc Bekoff, an evolutionary biologist who has written many books about the emotional lives of animals. In his blog, Bekoff urges people to recognize that they are part of the animal kingdom and to treat our fellow animals with greater compassion.

Animal Legal Historical Center

www.animallaw.info/articles/ddusicacl.htm

Michigan State University's College of Law maintains this resource, which has information about animal cruelty laws in the United States and the European Union.

Inside the Animal Mind

www.pbs.org/wnet/nature/episodes/inside-the-animal-mind/introduction/2081/

This site introduces the three-part PBS series *Inside the Animal Mind*, originally broadcast on the PBS show *Nature*. Topics include stress and social interaction.

Mind & Brain/Animal Intelligence

http://discovermagazine.com/topics/mind-brain/animal-intelligence

Discover's Animal Intelligence page has links to dozens of articles about recent discoveries, written for ordinary people, not scientific experts.

Neuroscience for Kids

http://faculty.washington.edu/chudler/brainsize.html

This site offers easy-to-understand language and pictures that explain the structure and function of the brain. One section talks about brain size in humans and some species of animals.

"Self-Recognition in Apes"

www.youtube.com/watch?v=vJFo3trMuD8

This National Geographic Society video highlights evidence of thought and emotion in apes; much of the five-minute video shows a mirror self-recognition test, in which apes respond to their own reflections.

Surprisingly Human

http://animal.discovery.com/videos/almost-human-chimps-human-tools.html

This collection of videos from the Animal Planet television channel features primatologist Jane Goodall and the chimpanzees she has spent decades studying. Topics include laughter and death.

BIBLIOGRAPHY

The author found these books and articles especially helpful.

Balcombe, Jonathan. *Second Nature: The Inner Lives of Animals*. New York: Palgrave Macmillan, 2010.

Bekoff, Marc. *Animal Passions and Beastly Virtues*. Philadelphia: Temple University Press, 2006.

——. *The Emotional Lives of Animals*. Novato, CA: New World Library, 2007.

——. *Minding Animals: Awareness, Emotions, and Heart*. New York: Oxford University Press, 2003.

Bekoff, Marc, and Jessica Pierce. *Wild Justice: The Moral Lives of Animals*. Chicago: University of Chicago Press, 2009.

Braithwaite, Victoria. *Do Fish Feel Pain?* New York: Oxford University Press, 2010.

Brown, Culum, and others, eds. *Fish Cognition and Behavior*. Ames, IA: Wiley-Blackwell, 2006.

Burkhardt, Richard W., Jr. *Patterns of Behavior: Konrad Lorenz, Niko Tinbergen, and the Founding of Ethology*. Chicago: University of Chicago Press, 2005.

Coghlan, Andy. "Whales boast the brain cells that 'make us human.'" New Scientist. November 27, 2006. www.newscientist.com/article/dn10661-whales-boast-the-brain-cells-that-make-us-human.html

Darwin, Charles. *The Expression of the Emotions in Man and Animals*. Cambridge, UK: Cambridge University Press, 2009. Originally published 1872.

Dawkins, Marian Stamp. "Animal Minds and Animal Emotions." *Journal of Integrative and Comparative Biology* 40, no. 6 (2000), 883–88, http://icb.oxfordjournals.org/content/40/6/883.full

Delude, Cathryn M. "Birds' brains reveal source of songs." *MIT News*. April 22, 2005. http://web.mit.edu/newsoffice/2005/songbirds.html

de Waal, Frans. *The Ape and the Sushi Master: Cultural Reflections of a Primatologist*. New York: Basic Books, 2001.

Fetzer, James H. *The Evolution of Intelligence: Are Humans the Only Animals with Minds?* Peru, IL: Carus, 2005.

LiveScience. "Fish Feel Pain, Study Finds." *LiveScience*. April 30, 2009. www.livescience.com/animals/090430-fish-feel-pain-too.html

Gould, James, and Carol Grant Gould. *Animal Architects: Building and the Evolution of Intelligence*. New York: Basic Books, 2007.

Griffin, Donald R. *Animal Minds: From Cognition to Consciousness*. 2nd ed. Chicago: University of Chicago Press, 2001.

Grimm, David. "Is a Dolphin a Person?" Science Now. Febraury 21, 2010. http://news.sciencemag.org/sciencenow/2010/02/is-a-dolphin-a-person.html

Harmon, Katherine. "Do Chimpanzees Understand Death?" *Scientific American*. April 27, 2010. www.scientificamerican.com/article.cfm?id=chimpanzees-understand-death

Hatkoff, Amy. *The Inner World of Farm Animals*. New York: Stewart, Tabori, & Chang, 2009.

Konkel, Lindsey. "Ants, All for One!" *Natural History*. November 2009, 14.

Linden, Eugene. *The Octopus and the Orangutan*. New York: Dutton, 2002.

Manning, Aubrey, and Marian Stamp Dawkins. *Animal Behavior*. 5th ed. Cambridge, UK: Cambridge University Press, 1998.

Marks, Kathy. "Save the whales: How Moko the dolphin came to the rescue of a mother and her calf." *The Independent*. March 13, 2008. www.independent.co.uk/ environment/nature/save-the-whales-how-moko-the-dolphin-came-to-the-rescue- of-a-mother-and-her-calf-795025.html

Masson, Jeffrey Moussaieff, and Susan McCarthy. *When Elephants Weep: The Emotional Lives of Animals*. New York: Dell, 1995.

McCarthy, Susan. *Becoming a Tiger: How Baby Animals Learn to Live in the Wild*. New York: HarperCollins, 2004.

O'Connell, Caitlin. *The Elephant's Secret Sense: The Hidden Life of the Wild Herds of Africa*. Chicago: University of Chicago Press, 2007.

Pitman, Robert L., and John W. Durban. "Save the Seal!" *Natural History*. November 2009, 48. www.naturalhistorymag.com/exploring-science-and-nature/161929/save- the-seal

Plotnik, Joshua M., Frans de Waal, and Diana Reiss. "Self-recognition in an Asian elephant." *Proceedings of the National Academy of Sciences* 103, no. 45. November 7, 2006. 17053–57. http://www.pnas.org/content/103/45/17053.full

Reiss, Diana, and Lori Marino. "Mirror self-recognition in the bottlenose dolphin: A case of cognitive convergence." *Proceedings of the National Academy of Sciences*. 98, no. 10, May 8, 2001. 5937–42. www.pnas.org/content/98/10/5937.full

Rödl, Thomas, and others. "Tameness and stress physiology in a predator-naive island species confronted with novel predation threat." *Proceedings of the Royal Society*. (2007) 274, 577–82. www.princeton.edu/~wikelski/Publications/2006%20 Roedl%20et%20al.%20Marine%20iguana%20tameness.pdf

Sapolsky, Robert. *A Primate's Memoir: A Neuroscientist's Unconventional Life Among the Baboons.* 3rd ed. New York: Scribner, 2002.

Society for Neuroscience. "Mirror neurons." *Brain Briefings.* November 2008. www.sfn.org/index.aspx?pagename=brainBriefings_MirrorNeurons

Uhlenbroek, Charlotte, ed. *Animal Life.* New York: Dorling Kindersley, 2008.

Wasserman, Edward A., and Thomas R. Zentall, eds. *Comparative Cognition: Experimental Explorations of Animal Intelligence.* New York: Oxford University Press, 2009.

Wynne, Clive. *Do Animals Think?* Princeton, NJ: Princeton University Press, 2004.
————. *Animal Cognition: The Mental Lives of Animals.* New York: Palgrave, 2001.

INDEX

Page numbers in **boldface** are photographs.